Oxford in Colour

by Levi Fox

'And now Oxford . . . She has to be understood and she deserves to be appreciated. She has nurtured, willingly or reluctantly, every element in our national life and in our work overseas. She has inspired great poetry, great prose, great music. Her buildings at their noblest are shrines of the arts. Her libraries give shelter to the lore of the ages. Her beauty can both soothe and exalt the minds of her children.'

SIR MAURICE POWICKE

Of books on Oxford there is no end. No place has provided a happier hunting ground for the local historian and antiquary or a more romantic theme for the novelist and poet. Diarists, travellers, scholars and journalists, no less than educationalists, architects, town planners, and speculators in general have all found here a subject of inexhaustible fascination. In the inspiration of volumes of reminiscences and eulogies, Oxford is without rival and no city has had its buildings more consistently sketched, painted and photographed.

What then can a publication like this hope to achieve? Certainly not to contribute anything new; but rather to provide in a convenient, modestly-priced format an introductory appreciation of some aspects of this famous university city and to convey through a selection of illustrations of representative scenes and buildings something of its character, atmosphere and charm.

Oxford is a rare jewel, priceless in itself, but enhanced by the richness of its setting. 'Oxford stands lowe', wrote a Jacobean judge in 1603, 'with rich meadowes about the rivers that runne by it: and . . . is invironed with pretie litle hills two miles off by south and west'. It is the natural centre of the rich, well-watered tract of pastoral and agricultural land lying in the upper basin of the Thames, and owed its origin and early development, in the first place, to its strategic and commercial importance, and from the twelfth century, to the seat of learning which became established there. Throughout the centuries Oxford has been a busy market town with a variety of useful domestic trades, a vital centre of road and river communications, the scene of an annual fair (still perpetuated in St Giles's fair), the headquarters of city and county government and justice, as well as the political, intellectual and social centre of the county. It has at present a resident population of nearly 120,000, and to this should be added students and tourists as well as those living in the surrounding area who regard the city as their natural centre for work, shopping and entertainment.

On the economic side Oxford has for centuries been famous for its printing, book-binding, publishing and beer-brewing, while in modern times it has become the centre of large-scale motor manufacture and allied products. Electrical switchgear, computers, scientific and medical equipment, furniture and boats are also made here. But to the world Oxford is famous as a beautiful university city, which takes its place, with London and Stratford-upon-Avon, as one of Britain's most popular tourist centres.

Its beginnings can be traced back over a thousand years. According to tradition St Frideswide founded a nunnery here in the eighth century and the place was of sufficient importance to have been mentioned with London in a document in the year 912. Commanding a fordable point on the River Thames on the border of Mercia and Wessex, Oxford played a part in the defence of the Thames valley against the Danes and following the Norman Conquest became a garrison town, fortified with a castle, wall and moat. The remains of the Norman castle – a great mound of earth, a stone tower and a chapel crypt – standing in the grounds of the prison survive as a physical link with the days of the first Norman governor, Robert D'Oiley, and recall the episode of Queen Matilda's escape from the castle by night to Wallingford when King Stephen laid siege to it in 1141. Part of the medieval city wall is preserved in New College gardens.

To this same period the beginnings of the University can be traced. Exactly why or when the first scholars settled here are matters of speculation, but an exodus of English students from the University of Paris in 1167 seems to have given an impetus to Oxford's growing popularity as a centre of learning; and by the end of the twelfth century its University, by which should be understood a corporation of teachers rather than a building, was in existence. A glimpse of the scholars is revealed to us in 1209 when a quarrel occurred between them and the town authorities, resulting in a dispersal of some of the students and masters to Cambridge. The first evidence of the presence of schools at

Cambridge dates from this migration from Oxford, though naturally Cambridge men are reluctant to concede this parentage.

At first students and masters lived in hired lodgings and used the parish churches for their lectures and schools; from this developed the practice whereby a group of students resided in a hall presided over by a master; finally, towards the end of the thirteenth century, Walter de Merton, founder of Merton College, set the pattern of later collegiate arrangements by establishing a college of scholars who lived and studied according to the rules prescribed by their founder. By the middle of the fifteenth century some ten colleges were in existence and by that time membership of one of these, or of a recognised hall, had become compulsory.

The privileges and status of the University also came to be defined and recognised, though not without a good deal of opposition from the townsmen. Fights between town and gown were frequent, the most celebrated being the riot which occurred on St Scholastica's Day, 1355. According to Anthony Wood there 'came Walter de Springhouse, Roger de Chesterfield, and other clerks, to the Tavern called Swyndlestock at Carfax, and there calling for wine, John de Croydon, the Vintner, brought them some, but they disliking it, as it should seem, and he avouching it to be good, several snappish words passed between them. At length the Vintner giving them stubborn and saucy language they threw the wine and vessel at his head. The Vintner, therefore, receding with great passion and aggravating the abuse to those of his family and neighbourhood, they caused the Town Bell at St Martin's to be rung that the Commonalty might be summoned together. Which being done, they in an instant were in arms, some with bows and arrows, others with divers sort of weapons. And then they without any more ado did in a furious and hostile manner, suddenly set upon divers Scholars, who at that time had not any offensive arms, no, not so much as anything to defend themselves. The Chancellor of the University, perceiving what great danger they were in, caused the University Bell at St Mary's to be rung out, whereupon the Scholars got bows and arrows, and maintained the fight with the Townsmen till dark night, at which time the fray ceased.' The battle was resumed the following day when the townsfolk, enlisting the help of the country folk, inflicted serious casualties on the scholars, only to find that their action had incurred the royal displeasure and that in consequence the University secured a considerable increase in its privileges.

There are now at Oxford thirty-five colleges and five halls. Twenty-eight of the colleges and the five halls take undergraduates while the other seven colleges are for graduates only; there are also several other educational institutions not directly linked with the University. In recent years women have come to be admitted to all the colleges which had hitherto been exclusively for men; but three colleges for women only still remain.

The colleges are autonomous corporations and each is an entity in itself, governed by its own statutes and traditions. Each college has its own governing body, administers its own estates and maintains its staff of tutors or 'dons'. Each college has its own hall, chapel, library, common rooms, lodgings and porter's lodge controlling access to its precincts. Each college regulates its own domestic life and provides for the physical, spiritual, intellectual and recreational well-being of its members. Each college has its own time-honoured arrangements, customs and ceremonies.

Yet the colleges are inseparable from the University in that membership of the one is an indispensable condition of admission to the other. The University provides a system of teaching over and above the colleges, with professors, readers and lecturers; it arranges the conduct of examinations, confers degrees and exercises disciplinary authority; it administers the Bodleian Library and the University Press and maintains various museums, literary and scientific departments. The University, in effect, is everywhere, though there is no specific building which can be pointed out as the University. The chief body responsible for the administration of the University is the Hebdomadal Council presided over by the Vice-Chancellor, but policy decisions require the approval of the larger legislative body known as Congregation.

Along with the colleges, the buildings associated with the University constitute Oxford's primary attraction. Of their architectural wealth some slight indication is afforded by the descriptions and illustrations which follow. Nowhere in England can the crafts of the stone mason, the carpenter and the glass painter be studied in such rich profusion. Oxford has representative examples of every style and period of building from Anglo-Saxon times to the present. Its architecture includes some of the most perfect examples of English medieval Gothic, together with specimens of the best achievements of stone statuary, wood carving, engraved memorials, decorative plaster, lead and iron work, and painted glass. Apart from the colleges, it has some good examples of domestic architecture, particularly in St Aldate's, the High Street, and Holywell Street, as well as ancient inns like the Mitre in High Street, the King's Arms in Holywell Street and the Golden Cross in Cornmarket Street with its cobbled yard

Magpie Lane, off High Street

where Shakespeare's plays may well have been performed.

Visitors with a short time at their disposal will do well to select a few sights rather than to attempt a hurried exploration of the whole. High Street, in preference to any other street, should be traversed from Magdalen Bridge to Carfax. Among colleges, Magdalen and Christ Church should come first, followed if possible by Merton, New College and St John's. Radcliffe Square should be visited with St Mary's Church, the Bodleian, the Divinity School, the Sheldonian Theatre and Ashmolean Museum. Individual taste must determine the rest but there is a goodly pick: St Michael's Church with its Saxon tower; the Norman crypt of St Peter-in-the-East Church; the Painted Room, formerly the guest chamber of the Crown Tavern where Shakespeare used to stay; All Souls College, the only college which has no undergraduates on its foundation; Worcester College with its garden and monastic buildings; Wadham College with its complete original buildings; Lincoln with its Wesley connection; St Catherine's College, founded 1962, designed by Arne Jacobsen; indeed any of the other colleges, for each has its own particular associations and points of architectural interest. Last but not least, a walk through Christ Church meadows to the river should be included. The beauty of the setting, the college boathouses and the practising eights and fours make an unforgettable scene.

Apart from its architecture and the beauty of its setting and surrounding country, Oxford is a city with a great history behind it. Frequently visited by reigning sovereigns, it has been linked with national events and movements which have now become part of the story of English history. Oxford men in their various spheres have advanced the study of their subjects and rendered incalculable services to their country and the world. No town, except London, can record a comparable succession of historical associations. To mention only a few, Oxford was the meeting place of royal and ecclesiastical councils in medieval times, the scene of the martyrdom of Ridley, Latimer and Cranmer (commemorated by the Martyrs' Memorial erected in 1841), the headquarters of King Charles I during the Civil War, and the source of the great religious movements associated with Wycliffe, Wesley and Newman.

Always receptive yet insular in its outlook, Oxford has in a sense acted as a barometer registering what Englishmen have thought and needed in successive generations. Steeped in tradition, occasionally perhaps prejudice, Oxford has been called the home of lost causes; yet it preserves its unique, unfailing fascination. History and antiquities, fine streets and buildings, beauty and charm are here in unstinted measure; but underlying all and far more important there are spiritual values which remain unchanged in the face of all conditions. Oxford represents a standard of scholarship, a sanity of judgement, a quality of behaviour and character which are the very essence of the English way of life and thought.

'The High'

Nowhere is the magnificence of Oxford better exemplified than in this lovely panoramic view of the High Street, the thoroughfare which runs east and west from Magdalen Bridge to the city centre at Carfax. Described by Carl Philipp Moritz, who visited Oxford in 1782, as 'the longest, the finest and the most beautiful street in Europe', it is certainly the most famous and most admired high street in England.

The charm of 'the High' derives at once from the graceful sweep of its curves and the variegated panorama of fine buildings which unfolds on either side. From whatever point the street is viewed it presents a striking vista of beauty. In no single street is there greater diversity of architectural styles; yet a more harmonious composition would be difficult to imagine.

In a real sense the High Street is characteristic of all the elements of town and gown which go to the making of present-day Oxford. Beyond St Martin's Tower at Carfax, itself an imposing feature, lies Queen Street (*top right*) and the busy Westgate Shopping Centre (*bottom right*).

To the north of Carfax runs Cornmarket Street, now closed to through traffic. Here are shops in variety including the arcade called the Clarendon Centre built in recent years. Oxford's Town Hall is situated in St Aldate's to the south of Carfax. Beyond is Folly Bridge which gives access to the towpath of the Isis or River Thames.

In the High itself hotels and houses, shops and offices, stand side by side with colleges and University buildings; there are two churches, the city Church of All Saints and the University Church of St Mary the Virgin; quiet narrow lanes with cobbled surfaces and still bearing their medieval names lead from the main street, where the busy traffic of modern transport intermingles with the throng of people, themselves representative of residents, students and academic folk, as well as visitors who come in increasing numbers to see the university city.

Colleges which abut on to 'the High' include Magdalen, Queen's, All Souls, Brasenose, University and Oriel. St Mary's Church, the focal point of university life from earliest times, is notable for its glorious tower and spire, which has aptly been described as 'the lordliest in England' and a 'miracle in art'. From this point the High follows a gentle curve eastwards down to Magdalen Bridge and tower. The River Cherwell as seen from the bridge is particularly beautiful and provides a perfect setting for the magnificent tower and college buildings. Nor should the visitor miss the Botanic Garden across the road from Magdalen.

The High from Magdalen Tower

St Martin's Tower, Carfax

All Saints Church

Examination Schools

University Church of St Mary the Virgin

Radcliffe Camera

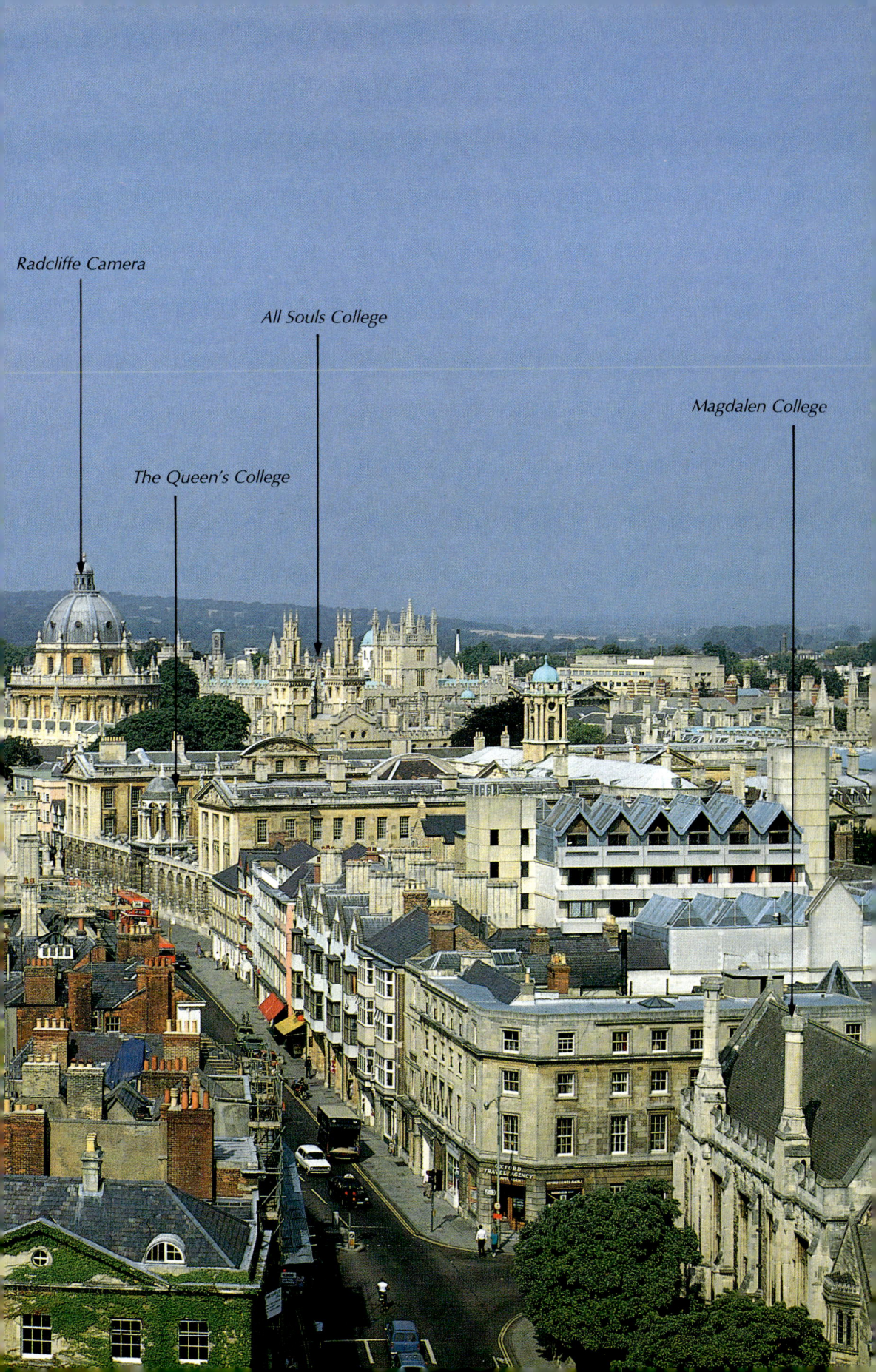

All Souls College

Magdalen College

The Queen's College

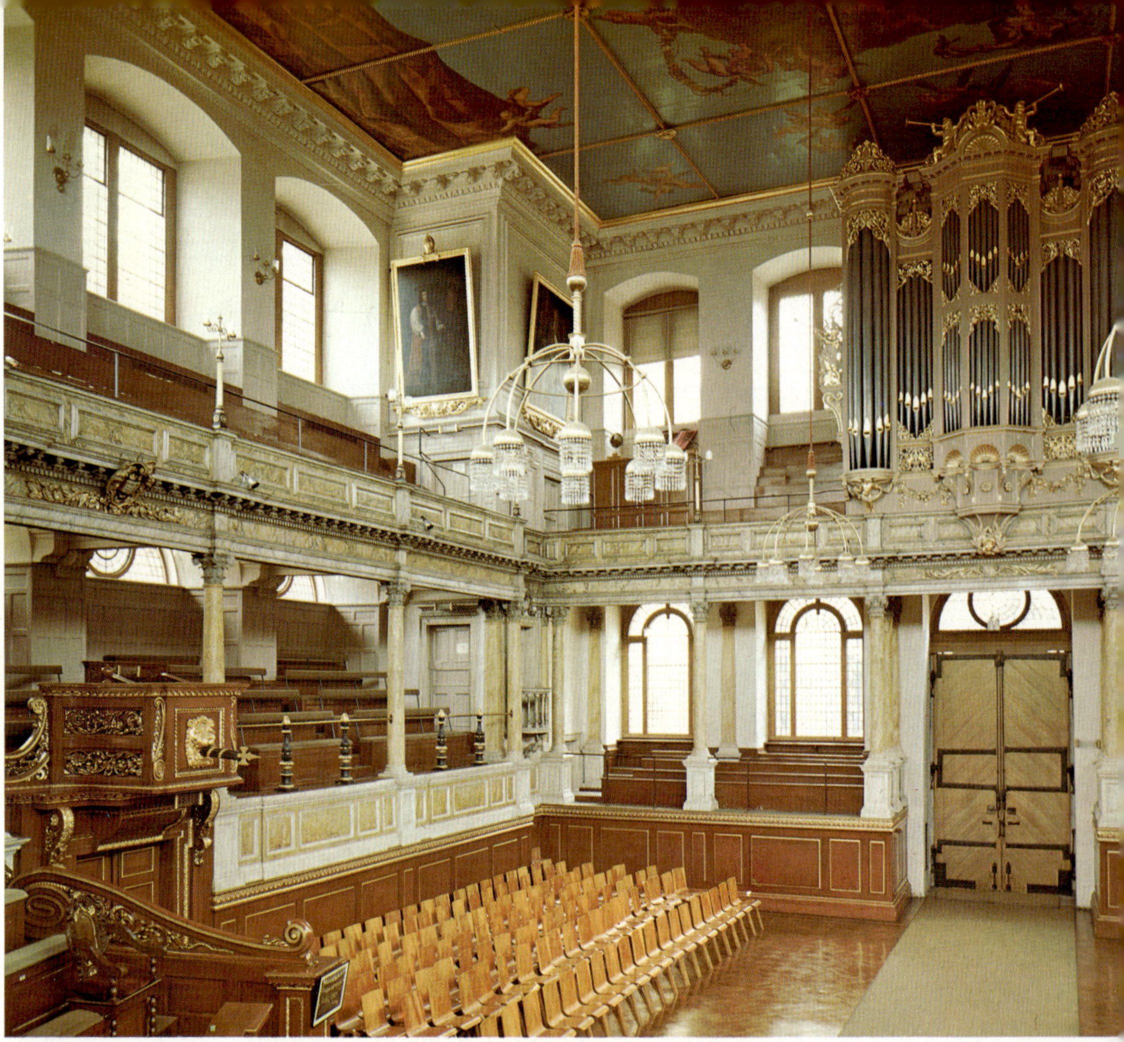

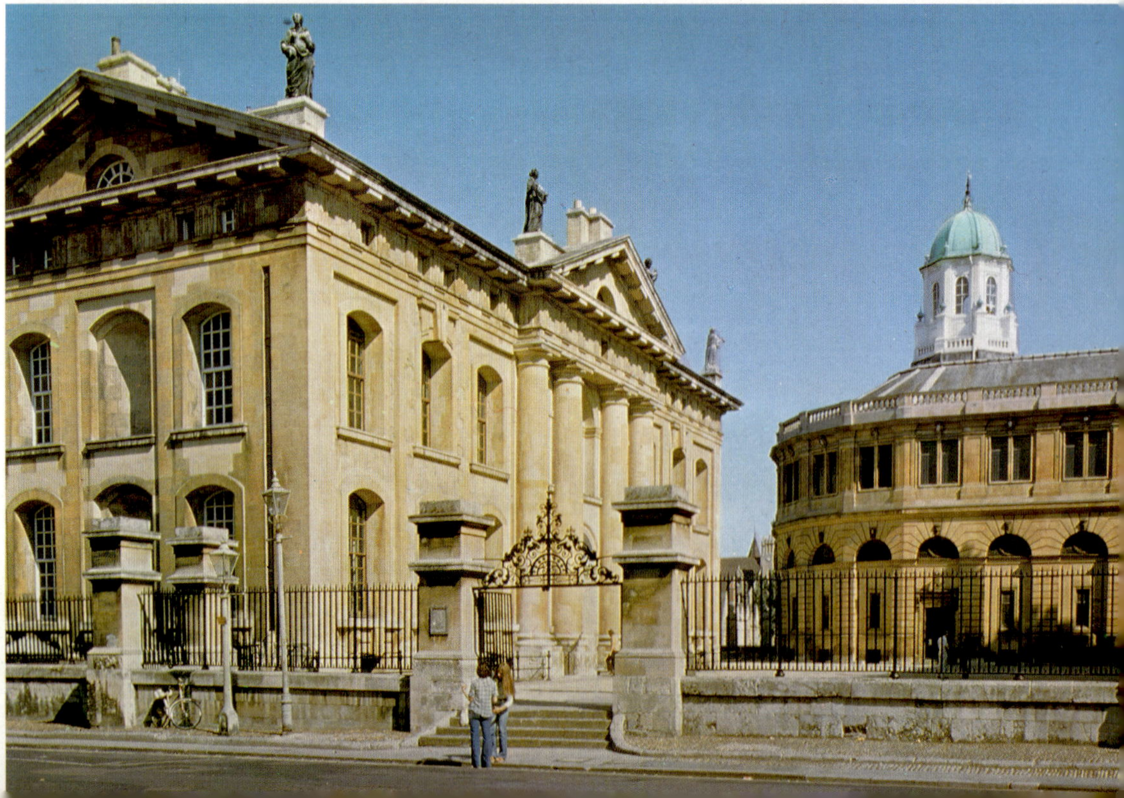

The Sheldonian Theatre

Next to the Bodleian Library and the Divinity School which stand nearby, the Sheldonian Theatre ranks as the most interesting of the University buildings. An early example of the work of Christopher Wren, this almost semicircular building contains many unusual features not found elsewhere in Oxford and it is the earliest surviving structure of its type in this country.

Built to the designs of Wren during the years 1664–69, the Sheldonian Theatre takes its name from Gilbert Sheldon, Archbishop of Canterbury, who defrayed the cost of building it to accommodate the University ceremonies which up till then had taken place in the University Church of St Mary, as well as to provide a home for the University Press.

The Sheldonian continues to be the scene of University ceremonies, the most notable being the *Encaenia* when honorary degrees are conferred by the Chancellor or Vice-Chancellor on distinguished persons.

Most striking is the interior of the theatre (*top left*) with its vast, apparently unsupported flat ceiling, a triumph of the mathematical genius of Wren. It is fashioned like a canvas awning strung upon ropes stretched from side to side and adorned with a galaxy of allegorical figures painted by Robert Streater (1624–80). The interior is divided into two main stages with a curious arrangement of tier-seating, galleries, boxes and chairs all designed for University ceremonies. The handsome organ case was designed by Sir T. G. Jackson (1877).

Nearby, the Clarendon Building (*below left*), the work of Nicholas Hawksmoor, was the home of the University Press from 1713 to 1829, when it transferred to Walton Street.

St Mary's Church

The present building, the third if not the fourth to be erected on the same site, is mostly in the Perpendicular style of the fifteenth century. The nave (*above*) and chancel were rebuilt between 1463 and 1490, but Adam de Brome's chapel on the north side dates from 1328.

As the University church St Mary's has important historical associations. It was the scene of the famous riots between town and gown in 1355 which resulted in royal confirmation of the University's authority; Bishops Ridley, Latimer and Cranmer stood trial here in 1555–56 before being burned to death at the stake; Wesley, the founder of Methodism, preached here, as also, later, Keble and Newman who inspired the Oxford Movement.

St Mary's was formerly used for University meetings and ceremonies. Today, during Full Term, the University Sermon, attended by the Vice-Chancellor and Proctors, is preached here.

QVOD FELICITER VORTAT
ACADEMICI OXONIENS
BIBLIOTHECAM HANC
VOBIS REIPVBLICAEQVE
LITERATORVM
T. B. P.

BODLEIAN LIBRARY

The Bodleian Library

The Bodleian ranks as the greatest library in the world, and is of outstanding interest and importance not merely because of the wealth of its printed and manuscript collections but also because of its history as an institution and the character of its buildings.

The library was founded soon after the middle of the fifteenth century to accommodate books given to the University by Humphrey, Duke of Gloucester, and the portion of the Bodleian known as Duke Humphrey's Library goes back to that date. Practically the whole of this early library collection was destroyed or dispersed by King Edward VI's commissioners in 1550, but the library was restored and rearranged by Sir Thomas Bodley (*opposite*) and re-opened in 1602.

Bodley conferred a lasting privilege on the University by arranging an agreement with the Stationers' Company that one copy of every book published in Great Britain should be sent to the Bodleian, a privilege which it still enjoys as a copyright library.

Bodley's munificence also made possible the provision of the three ranges of buildings comprising the Schools Quadrangle adjoining during the years 1613–18. As indicated by the names over the doorways inside the quadrangle these buildings were designed and used for teaching and examination purposes by the various schools and faculties comprising the University, but all of them have now been absorbed into the library.

The view of the library from the south-east, framed between All Souls on the right and the Radcliffe Camera on the left, emphasises the dignified proportions of these lofty Jacobean buildings.

An extension to the Bodleian Library, designed by Sir Giles Gilbert Scott, was built at the corner of Broad Street in 1937–40. It is connected to the old library by an underground passage.

The Radcliffe Camera

The conspicuous domed building known as the Radcliffe Camera (*above*) rises majestically in the middle of Radcliffe Square, surrounded on every side by historic academic buildings.

Built between 1737 and 1749 as a Physic Library for Dr John Radcliffe, Queen Anne's physician, the Camera was designed by the well-known English architect, James Gibbs, to whom Cambridge owes its Senate House and London the Church of St Martin-in-the-Fields.

Since 1861 the Camera has been used as a reading room of the Bodleian, providing facilities particularly for undergraduates requiring more modern publications.

The Botanic Garden

In his informative and entertaining *An Oxford University Chest* the late poet laureate, Sir John Betjeman, wrote: 'Of a summer afternoon ·when the splash of punt poles is heard on the Cherwell and the High Street traffic is deadened by the intervening architecture, and as Magdalen Tower, looking its best, strikes the quarters, I recommend a walk in the Botanic Garden.'

Situated alongside the Cherwell (*opposite*), a river popular for its punting and recreational appeal, the Botanic Garden came into existence originally as the Physick Garden associated with the Faculty of Medicine.

The site was given to the University by Henry Danvers, Earl of Danby, in 1621 and is enclosed by a high ashlar stone wall. The approach from a point opposite Magdalen College is dominated by a baroque entrance gateway by Nicholas Stone, 1586–1647 (*top left*). A bust of Danvers surmounts the arch and statues of Charles I and Charles II occupy the niches at the side.

It is said that the first gardener, a German, Jacob Bobart from Brunswick, collected 3,000 plants of different kinds; today the garden is notable for the interest of its wealth of trees and plants, established and developed over the years. There are also glass houses containing rare botanic specimens.

Examination Schools

Within a few yards distance the Elizabethan-style building known as the Examination Schools in High Street was built in 1882 to the design of Sir Thomas Jackson, R.A. It also has a quadrangle frontage in Merton Street (*below left*).

During term time the Schools are regularly used for lectures and it is here that undergraduates take their final degree examinations.

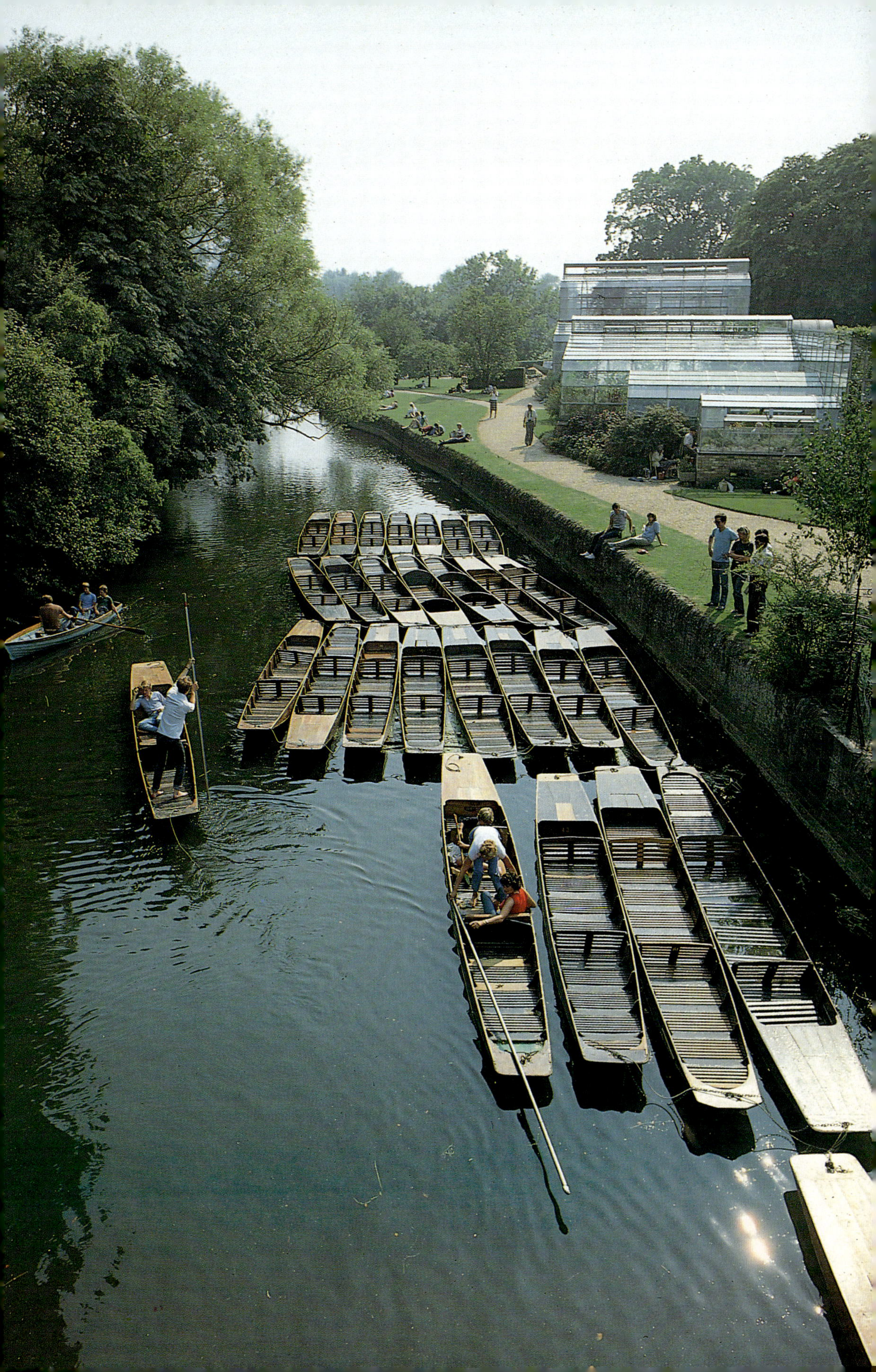

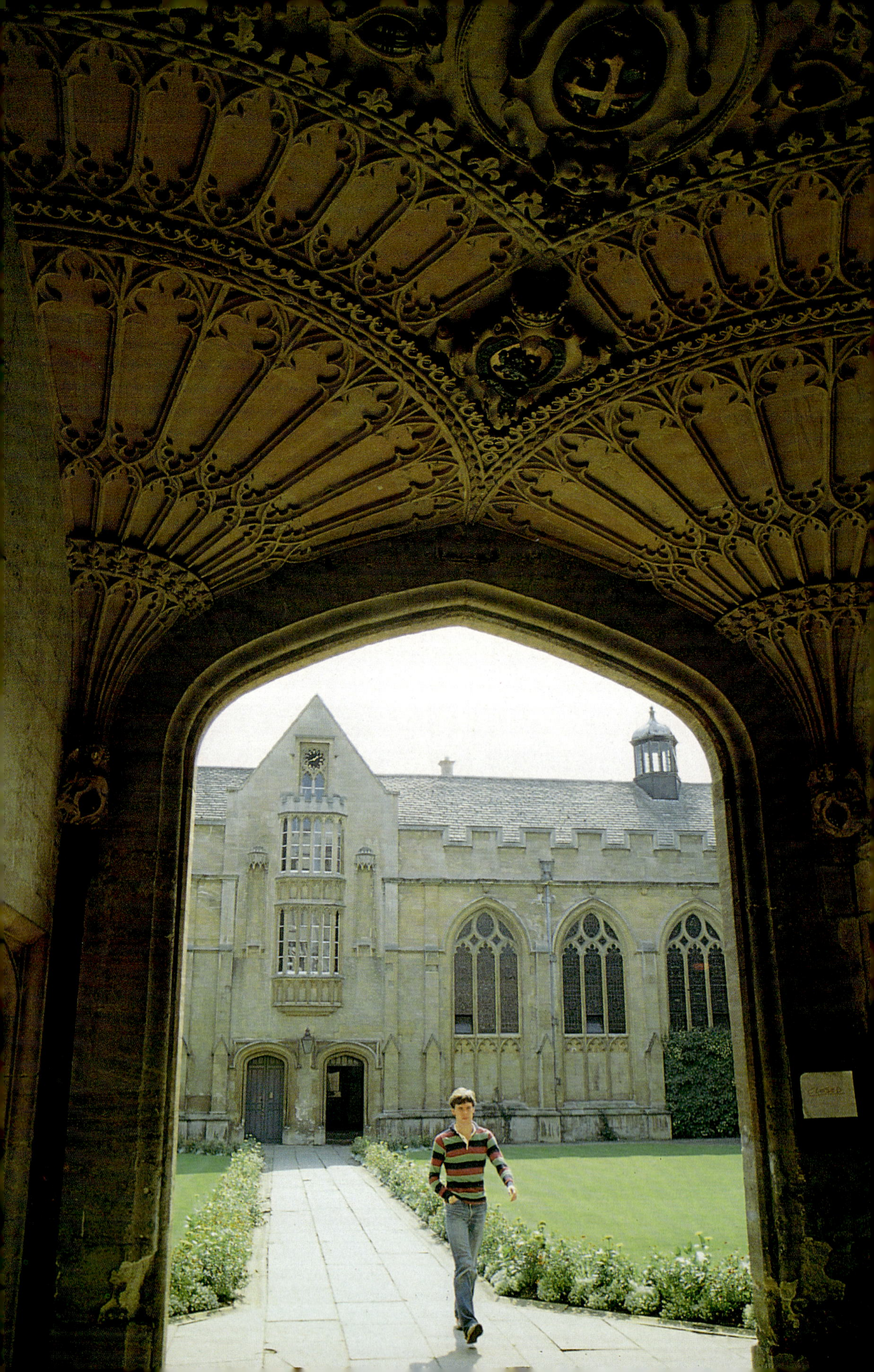
CLOSED

University College

Along with Merton and Balliol, University College (*right*) claims to be the oldest collegiate foundation in Oxford. Traditionally its origin is attributed to King Alfred but its historical endowment dates from 1249 when William of Durham gave money to the University for the maintenance of ten or more Masters of Arts to study theology.

There is evidence that the college buildings in the fifteenth century included a gatehouse, a hall, kitchen and chapel; all these were rebuilt during the seventeenth century. The Radcliffe Quadrangle was built between 1716 and 1719 and later additions are in the traditional Gothic style.

The college has several notable features: the seventeenth-century carved stalls and screen in the chapel, together with the glass by Abraham van Linge, 1641; the fan vaulting (*left*) in the porches of the larger and smaller quadrangles; the fine early panelling and carving in the Summer Common Room; and the Shelley Memorial by Onslow Ford in the first quadrangle.

Over the archway of the main gate, facing the High, is a statue of Queen Anne.

Balliol College

Notable for its outstanding record of academic achievement and its influence on English national life for more than a century, Balliol College (*below*) was founded by John Balliol towards the end of the thirteenth century.

Although much of the college was rebuilt in the nineteenth century, interesting medieval portions remain, particularly the old hall, now the library and the upper library.

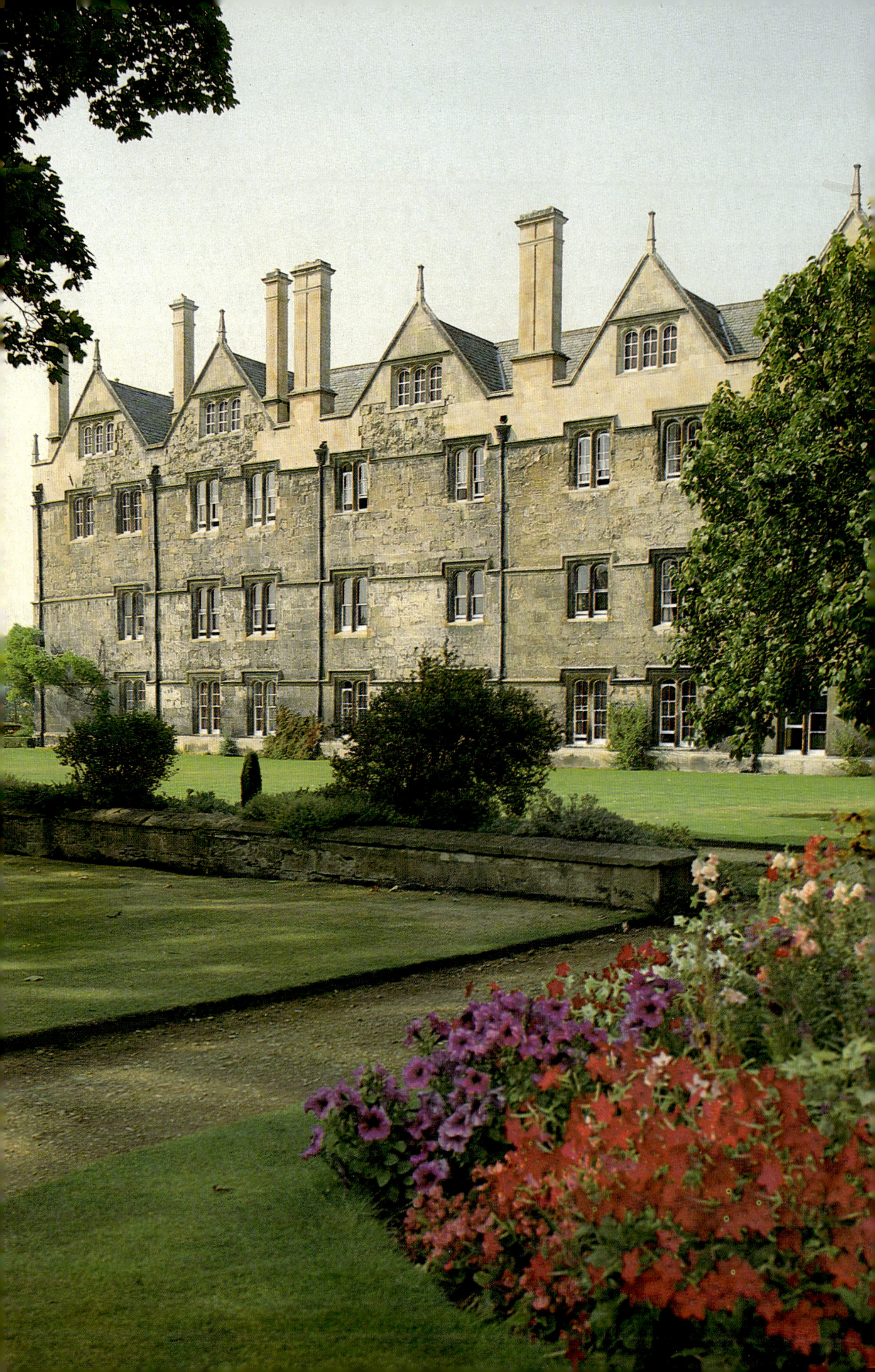

Merton College

Founded in 1224 by Walter de Merton, later Bishop of Rochester, Merton (*left*) enjoys the distinction of being the oldest college in Oxford. Though the grouping of the college buildings is the most irregular of all the Oxford colleges, it presents the earliest example of collegiate planning, which was used and improved upon by all later founders. Several of its buildings go back to the early days of the college and possess individual features of special interest. The college accounts begin in 1287.

The college chapel, which also served as the Parish Church of St John the Baptist, is a fine combination of the early Gothic styles. The choir is notable for the magnificent decorated tracery of its east window, the rare contemporary glass, the carved sedilia, monuments and floor-slabs. The tower is a lovely specimen of the Perpendicular style.

The library nearby also claims special attention. Built between the years 1371–79, it is the oldest of the college libraries and still largely preserves its original character. In it may be seen one of the original bookcases with its chained books.

Oriel College

Founded in 1324 by Adam de Brome, Rector of St Mary's, the college recognises as its titular founder Edward II, whose statue appears with that of Charles I over the porch on the steps leading to the hall (*top right*).

The medieval buildings were rebuilt between 1620 and 1642 and the first quadrangle is an attractive example of the Gothic style then used. The roofs and fittings of the hall and chapel are noteworthy.

The Rhodes building facing the High commemorates the association of Cecil Rhodes with the college. A portrait of him may be seen in the dining hall.

St Edmund Hall

Hard by the ancient church of St Peter-in-the-East, noteworthy for its fine vaulted Norman crypt, stands St Edmund Hall, the only surviving medieval hall in Oxford, though now enjoying the status of a college.

It has a charming miniature quadrangle (*above*) and collegiate buildings. The chapel and library were built in 1680–82.

New College

New College, founded in 1379 by William of Wykeham, Bishop of Winchester as a college 'new' in its architectural conception as well as in its academic method, is deservedly regarded as one of the show colleges of Oxford. For here may be seen a grouping of buildings in a lovely setting preserved substantially in the form in which they were designed by the founder.

The college was officially opened in 1386, by which time the main buildings, including the gatehouse, the hall, chapel and rooms in the great quadrangle, had been completed. The cloisters and bell tower, commenced a few years later, were finished by 1400.

The chapel and cloisters (*top left*) stand very high in the list of Oxford's architectural beauties. The chapel comprises a wide ante-chapel set at right angles to the choir and its crowning glory is its fourteenth-century painted glass. The cloisters, standing to the west of the chapel, were built by the founder.

All Souls College

Founded by Henry Chichele, Archbishop of Canterbury, in 1437, All Souls (*left*) is different from all the other colleges, with the exception of the modern foundations of Nuffield and St Antony's, because it still preserves the medieval custom of accepting graduates only.

The college possesses a fine quadrangle almost unchanged since the founder's time, together with two other quadrangles displaying a diversity of later styles. The chapel contains a magnificent classical screen and misericords of mid-fifteenth century date. Particularly impressive also is the Codrington Library noted for its collection of legal works and the striking twin towers designed by Nicholas Hawksmoor (1669–1745).

The Queen's College

Standing on the north side of High Street, the Queen's College (*right*) is especially noteworthy for its stately front quadrangle designed in the Palladian style by Nicholas Hawksmoor, a pupil of Wren.

The college was founded in 1340 by Robert de Eglesfield, chaplain to Queen Philippa, wife of Edward III. The medieval buildings were demolished and the college rebuilt on a larger scale between the years 1672 and 1760. The hall was finished in 1715 and the chapel shortly afterwards.

The most impressive building is the library (*below*) built between 1692 and 1695, exquisitely proportioned, embellished with a wealth of decorative plaster features and furnished with neatly balanced bookcases.

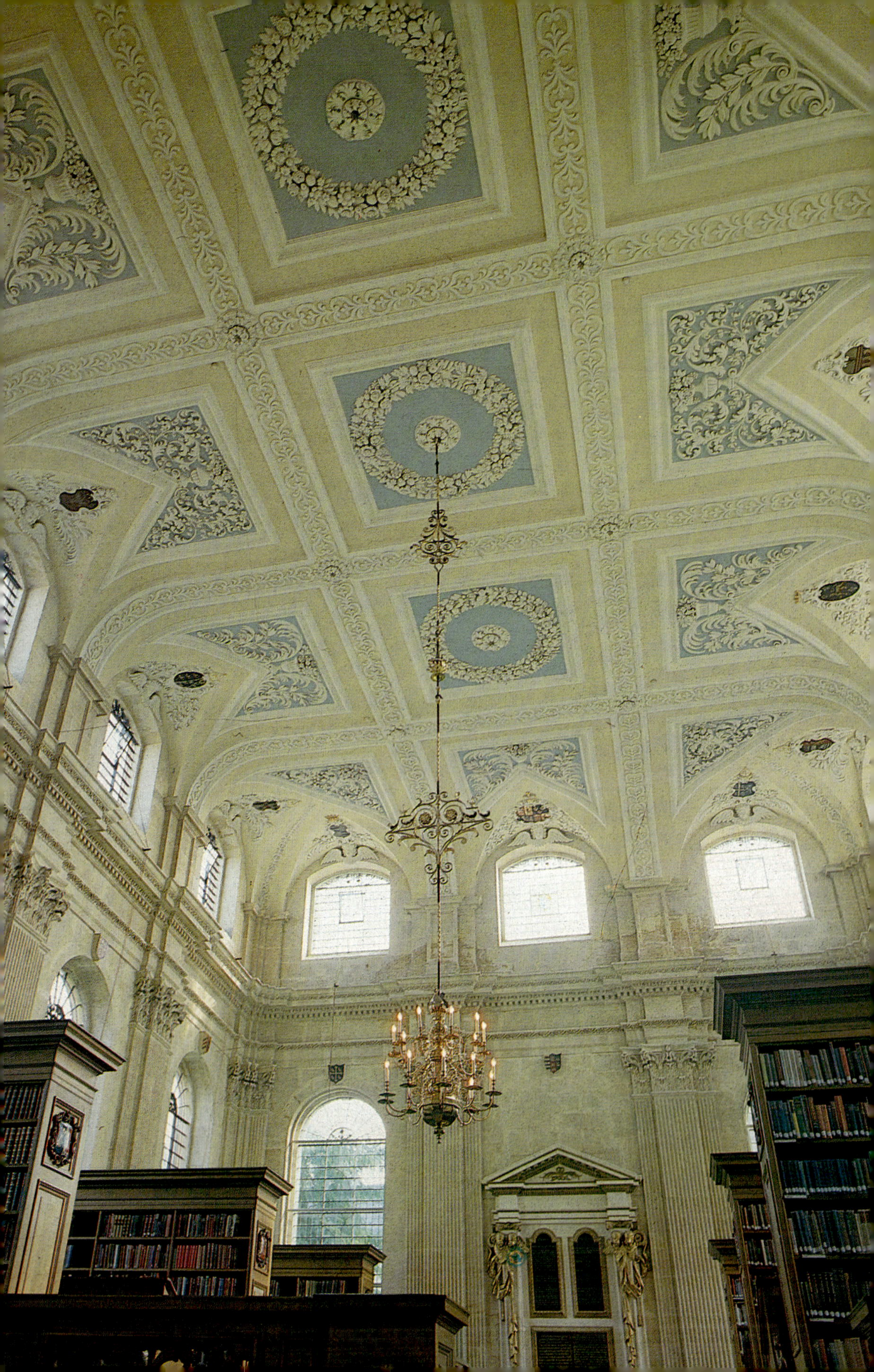

Lincoln College

Founded by Richard Fleming, Bishop of Lincoln, in 1427, and situated in the Turl, Lincoln College, though smaller than many of the colleges, is not lacking in interest. It possesses two small quadrangles, the first of which, with its simple gatehouse (*right*), was completed by 1437. The hall also dates back to this time; it contains some interesting medieval features, including the roof with its original octagonal louvre and a fireplace dating from 1699.

The seventeenth-century chapel contains remarkable woodwork, a large classic screen and contemporary glass by Abraham van Linge.

The college has had modern additions, which include the new library, 1906-7 (*opposite*) built in the garden and the new Rector's house, 1930, facing Turl Street.

The college's famous men include Sir William Davenant; Dr John Radcliffe, Physician, one of Oxford's great benefactors, who gave the Radcliffe Camera, the Radcliffe Observatory and Infirmary; and John Wesley, the founder of the non-conformist movement which bears his name.

St John's College

Incorporating the earlier Cistercian College of St Bernard, St John's College was founded by Sir Thomas White, one of the greatest of London's Lord Mayors, in 1555.

The early seventeenth-century Canterbury Quadrangle (*below*), is striking by reason of the central semi-circular archway feature set in relation to the well-proportioned arcading. In the niche above the arch stands one of the most notable ornaments of the period, a life-size bronze statue of Queen Henrietta Maria, consort of Charles I. The college is notable for its attractive garden with a fine lawn and rock garden.

Brasenose College

Occupying the site of earlier halls, Brasenose College (or B.N.C. as it is called), founded in 1509, is entered by a magnificent gate tower from Radcliffe Square (*above right*). The view immediately above is from the old quadrangle looking south-east with the Radcliffe Camera visible above the college buildings, of which the third-storey gables of early Jacobean date are a distinguishing feature.

The hall, standing on an undercroft, was probably built about the middle of the seventeenth century. The chapel is of the same period and displays a mixture of classical and Gothic features, with a fan tracery ceiling. The chapel stalls and lectern are of eighteenth-century date.

Brasenose has a distinguished reputation for rowing and sport.

Magdalen College

Anthony Wood asserted that Magdalen College (*opposite top*) was 'the most noble and rich structure in the learned world'. It is without question Oxford's loveliest college, set in an almost perfect setting beside the River Cherwell. Founded in 1458 by William of Waynflete, Bishop of Winchester, the college retains most of its original buildings largely complete, the chapel, hall, kitchen, cloisters and founder's tower being especially noteworthy.

Magdalen's outstanding ornament, however, is the Bell Tower, built between 1492 and 1509. The tower is of four storeys and five external stages, with octagonal turrets at each corner. As seen in the picture (*opposite top left*) it soars above the college buildings with an air of grace and beauty.

Corpus Christi College

One of the smaller colleges, founded in 1516 by Richard Fox, successively Bishop of Exeter, Bath and Wells, Durham and Winchester, Corpus Christi enjoys a reputation for scholarship. It has been described as 'rich out of all proportion to its size'.

In addition to its hall, chapel and cloister, the college has one of the most important libraries in Oxford, possessing many rare seventeenth-century books and manuscripts.

The view on the right shows the three-storey gatehouse with its embattled parapet and an unusual sundial in the middle of the quadrangle, erected in 1581. On the top is a pelican of 1581 date and a perpetual calendar was added to the pillar in 1606.

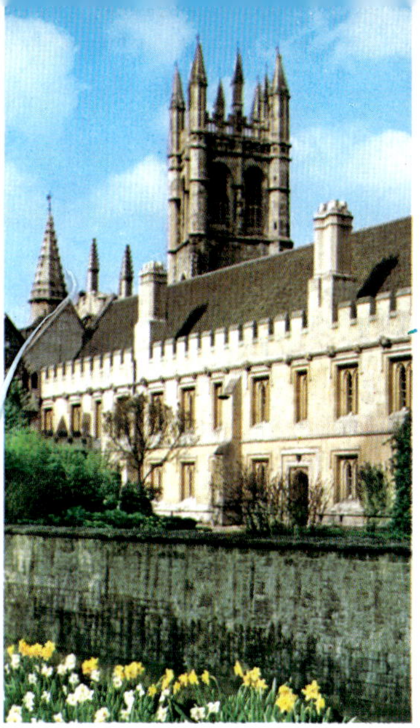

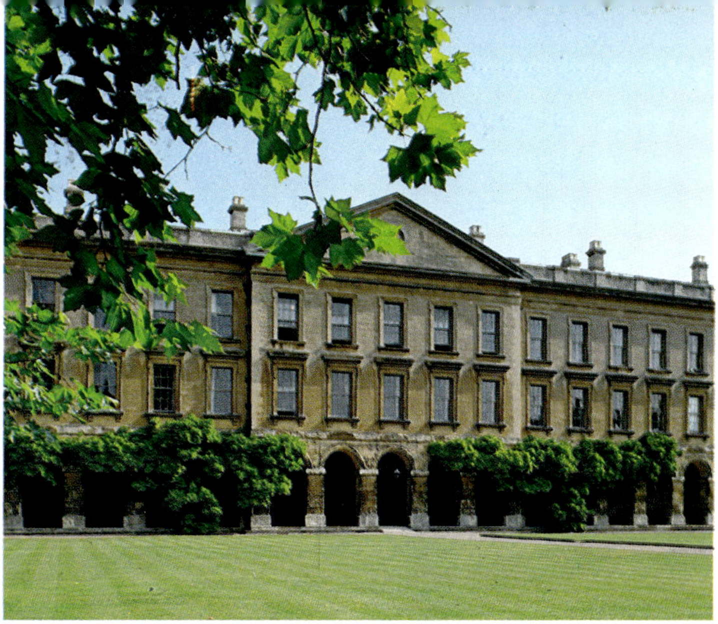

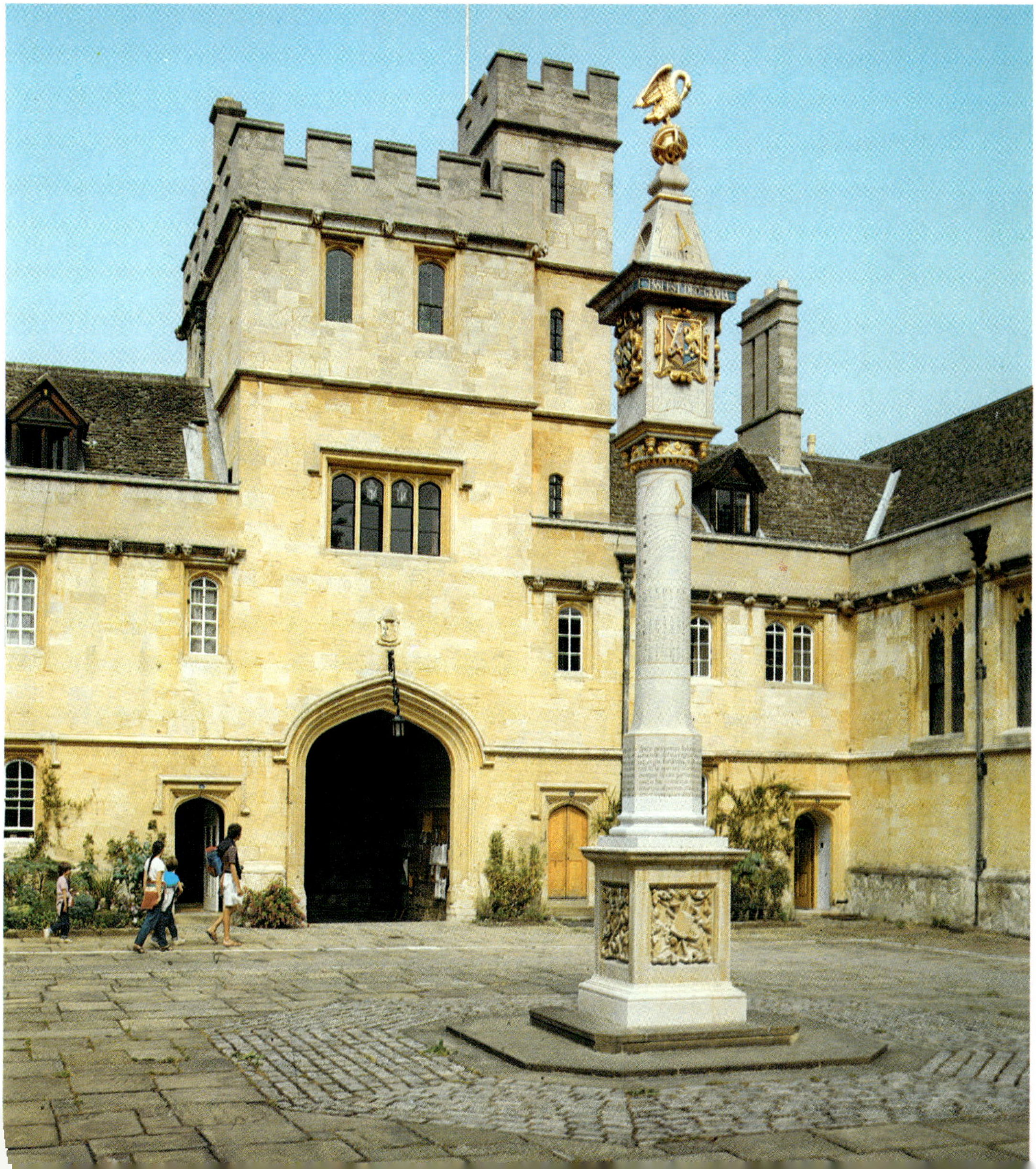

Christ Church

Christ Church is the biggest and most imposing of the Oxford colleges. First founded as Cardinal College by Cardinal Wolsey in 1525 on the site of the former priory of St Frideswide, the college was refounded after Wolsey's fall by King Henry VIII and subsequently completed.

Entrance from St Aldate's through the gateway under Tom Tower (*opposite top left*) leads to the Great Quadrangle, the size and grandeur of which are indicative of the grand conception of the founder's plan. The gateway was left unfinished by Wolsey and was completed by Christopher Wren in 1681–82. In the tower hangs the huge bell, known as Great Tom, which rings out a curfew of 101 strokes each night as a warning that the college gates are about to be closed.

The dining hall standing in the south-east corner of the quadrangle is unequalled in architectural excellence or historical association. Approached by a staircase famous for its fan-vaulted stone roof, the hall is a stately edifice of grand proportions with a superb hammerbeam roof of eight bays, completed in 1529.

Nearby is the college chapel (*opposite top right*) which now serves as the cathedral for the diocese of Oxford. Though among the smallest of English cathedrals it exhibits many features of special interest, such as the twelfth-century Norman pillars, its Early English spire and the exquisite fifteenth-century vaulting of the choir.

The library (*opposite bottom*) overlooking the Peckwater Quadrangle was built in 1716–61. The plasterwork of its interior and the craftsmanship of its furniture are particularly impressive.

Trinity College

Incorporating the buildings of Durham College which was suppressed at the time of the Reformation, Trinity College was established by Sir Thomas Pope in 1556.

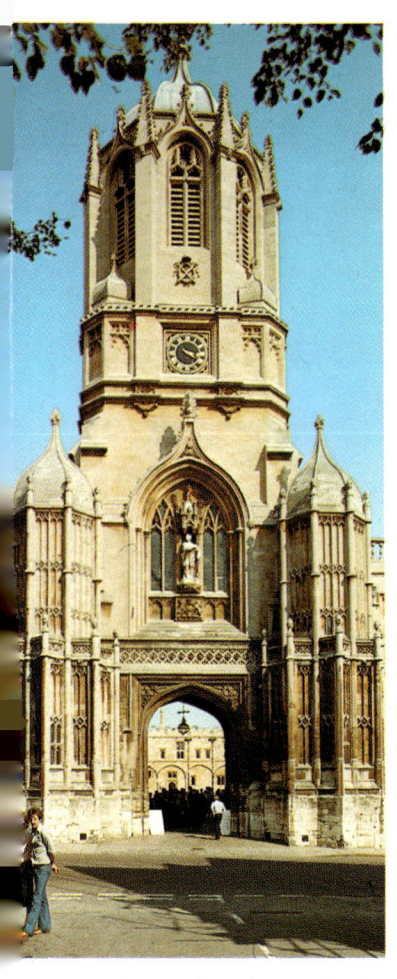

Its chief glory is the chapel (*opposite top*) built in 1691. It has a magnificent interior with a beautiful screen and altar-piece wood carving by Grinling Gibbons. The painting on the ceiling by Paul Berchet depicts the Ascension.

Jesus College
This college (*opposite bottom*) has always had close associations with Welsh students. It was founded officially by Queen Elizabeth I in 1571 at the instance of Dr Hugh Price. Its buildings are mostly of seventeenth-century date with later additions. The hall, library and chapel have interesting fittings.

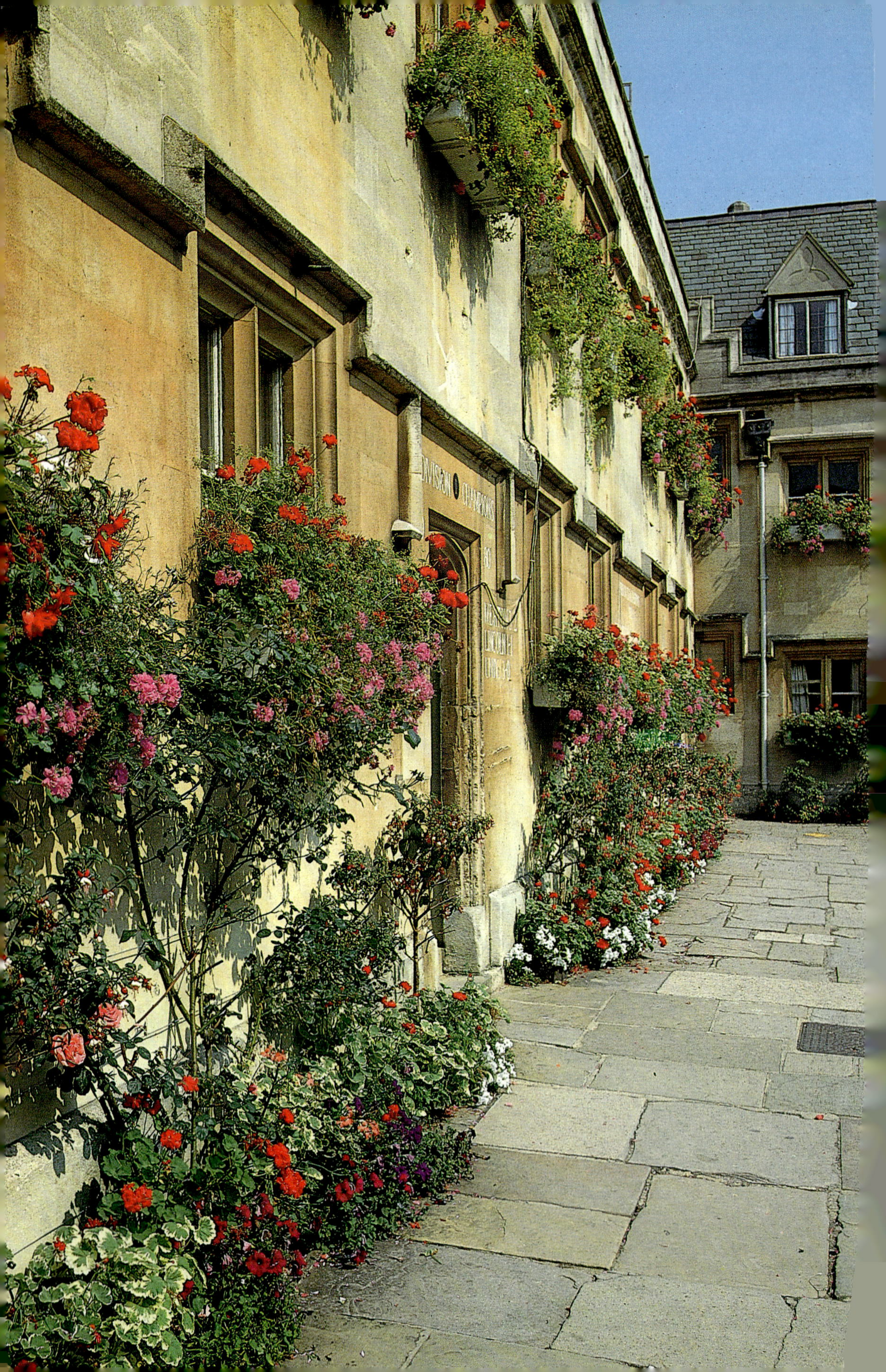

Pembroke College

When it was refounded in 1624 Pembroke College absorbed the medieval Broadgates Hall. Tucked away behind St Aldate's Church, the college has two quadrangles, the first of which is strikingly picturesque with its window boxes and Virginia creeper (*left*).

The Master's Lodgings date back to the sixteenth century, but the other buildings belong to the seventeenth century or later. On the second floor over the gate are the rooms occupied by Dr Samuel Johnson whose portrait by Reynolds is preserved in the Common Room. Here also is his teapot and the desk on which he compiled his famous dictionary.

Wadham College

Though one of the smallest and youngest colleges, Wadham is outstanding. Its buildings are of special interest not only as presenting a complete and little-altered original college layout and structure, but also as illustrating the fact that the Gothic style survived and was practised to perfection in Oxford when it was being rapidly superseded elsewhere.

Founded by Nicholas Wadham, a Somerset gentleman, and his wife Dorothy, who subsequently carried out his intentions, Wadham was built substantially in its present form during the years 1610 to 1613.

The main quadrangle, as illustrated by the central feature in the east range (*top right*), gives an excellent impression of the perfect symmetry of the buildings as a whole.

The hall (*right*) is one of the most striking in Oxford with a fine hammerbeam roof and original Jacobean woodwork. Equally satisfying from an architectural point of view is the chapel and antechapel, as seen from the park-like setting of the college garden, with the painted glass of the Dutchman, Bernard van Linge.

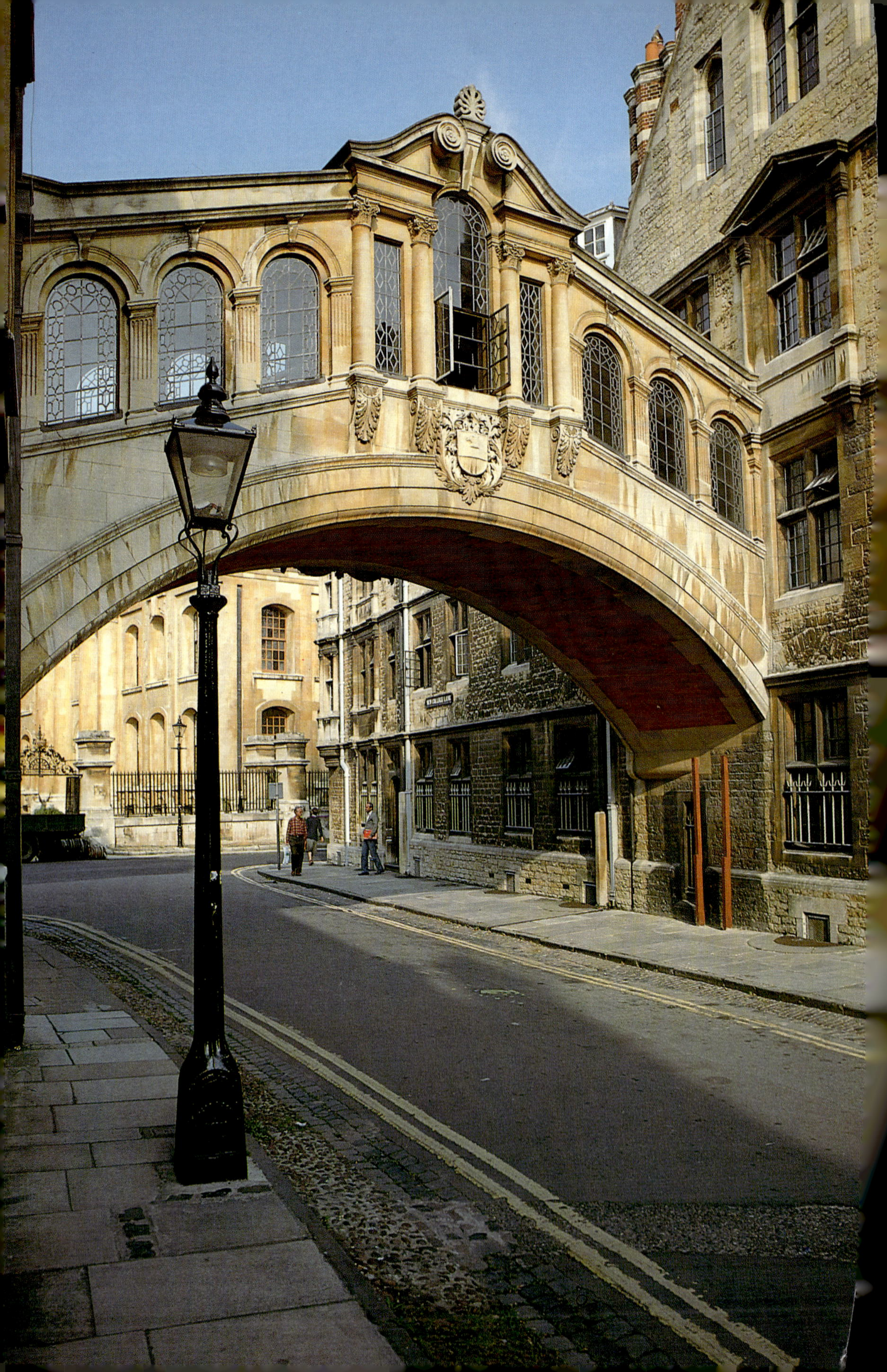

Hertford College

Situated opposite the Tower Gateway of the Bodleian Library, the buildings of Hertford College offer a mixture of architectural styles. They incorporate the late sixteenth-century old hall and buttery of Hart Hall and the buildings of later date which belonged to Magdalen Hall.

The college's most celebrated feature is the 'Bridge of Sighs' (*left*) constructed in 1913 to link newer buildings on the opposite side of the College Lane with the older complex.

Worcester College

Worcester College had its origins in Gloucester Hall, a college for Benedictine monks established in Oxford as early as 1298. After its suppression by King Henry VIII the buildings suffered various vicissitudes before being refounded as Worcester College in 1714 by Sir Thomas Cookes, Bart.

Most of the college buildings are of eighteenth-century date but a range of separate lodgings which originally belonged to Gloucester College remain (*top right*). They serve as a reminder of the residential arrangements of a medieval college, with each set of students' rooms being approached by a separate staircase.

The garden of Worcester is also noteworthy, for among Oxford gardens it stands next in beauty to St John's.

Keble College

Founded in memory of the Reverend John Keble, one of the leaders of the Oxford Movement, Keble College was the first college in Oxford to be built in brick. Designed by William Butterfield, its buildings (1870–78) display an unusual multi-patterned treatment of red, yellow and blue bricks with stone dressings.

The chapel (*right*) is the dominating feature. Here may be seen Holman Hart's famous painting, *The Light of the World*.

Lady Margaret Hall

It was not until the end of the last century that Oxford University opened its doors to women students. Lady Margaret Hall in north Oxford was established in 1878 for members of the Church of England and Somerville College was founded the following year as an inter-denominational college. St Hugh's followed in 1886, St Hilda's in 1893 and St Anne's in 1952.

The buildings of Lady Margaret Hall (*top left*) offer a pleasing variety of modern styles and the college garden runs down to the Cherwell.

Green College

This is one of Oxford's new colleges, opened in 1979 on a site adjoining the Radcliffe Infirmary. Incorporated in its buildings is the Radcliffe Observatory (*below left*) which was designed in 1772–5 by Henry Keene and James Wyatt to house the University's observatory instruments.

It is a pleasing building, the first built in Oxford under the influence of the Greek revival style. The college is devoted to medical research and was the gift of Dr and Mrs Cecil Green of Texas.

Nuffield College

Founded in 1937 by Viscount Nuffield who pioneered the mass production of the motor car and established the Morris manufacturing plant at Cowley. His intention was to encourage research in the field of social sciences at post-graduate level.

The college buildings of simple and traditional design stand on the site of the former canal wharf and castle wall at the junction of New Road and Worcester Street. The great tower with its copper-clad spire is a principal feature. The chapel has windows designed by John Piper, well-known because of his work at Coventry Cathedral. The college dining hall is illustrated opposite.

River Recreation

Of the full range of sports and recreational activities which flourish in the University none is more popular, or attracts more involvement, than rowing and punting, as illustrated in these pictures.

Every college has its own boat crew or crews which row regularly on the stretch of the Isis between Folly Bridge and Iffley Locks. Until a few years ago each college had its own floating barge which served as its boating headquarters but these have now given way to pavilion-type boathouses on the river bank.

In Hilary term inter-college races, known as Torpids, are rowed over this course for a period of four days and during Trinity term in summer Eights Week has become an established fixture in the University's sporting calendar. Eight-oared crews from all the colleges (*top left*) compete for the 'Head of the River' distinction. The college boats are positioned at equal distances along the river and at the starting signal each crew attempts to overtake the boat immediately in front and to 'bump' its stern. The boat which crosses the finishing line without being caught is the winner. It is not surprising that Eights Week has become a fashionable social occasion for undergraduates, parents and friends.

No less popular, but certainly more relaxing and less strenuous, is the leisurely recreation of punting on the Cherwell. The picture on the left illustrates a typical summer-day scene near to Magdalen Bridge. For those who prefer to walk perhaps the most popular route is along the towpath from Folly Bridge to Iffley village along the Thames.

ISBN 0–7117–0263–2
© 1987 Jarrold Colour Publications
Printed and published in Great Britain by
Jarrold and Sons Ltd, Norwich. 187